8/16

BATMAN

ADVENTURES OF THE
DARK KNIGHT

Written by Billy Wrecks

Batman created by Bob Kane

DK | Penguin Random House

Senior Editor Cefn Ridout
Senior Designer Robert Perry
Designer Chris Gould
Senior Pre-Production Producer Jennifer Murray
Producer Louise Daly
Managing Editor Sadie Smith
Managing Art Editor Ron Stobbart
Art Director Lisa Lanzarini
Publisher Julie Ferris
Publishing Director Simon Beecroft

Reading Consultant Linda B Gambrell

Design and additional text Rich T Media

First American Edition, 2016
Published in the United States by DK Publishing
345 Hudson Street, New York, New York 10014
DK, a Division of Penguin Random House LLC

16 17 18 19 20 10 9 8 7 6 5 4 3 2 1

001–280586–Feb/2016

DC COMICS™

A catalog record for this book
is available from the Library of Congress.

ISBN: 978-1-4654-4608-4 (Hardback)
ISBN: 978-1-4654-4609-1 (Paperback)

Printed and bound in China.

www.dk.com

A WORLD OF IDEAS
SEE ALL THERE IS TO KNOW

Contents

4 Who is the Dark Knight?

6 **Becoming Batman**

12 News flash!

14 **Personality and abilities**

20 **Armed and dangerous**

24 Utility Belt

28 Beyond the Batmobile

30 **Locations**

34 Secrets of the Batcave

38 Inside the Madhouse

40 **Fearsome foes**

68 Batman's greatest battles

70 **Awesome allies**

74 The many faces of Robin

84 Are you ready to join the Batman Family?

88 The Justice League

90 Quiz

92 Glossary

94 Index and Quiz Answers

Who is the Dark Knight?

Batman is the sworn guardian of Gotham City. Under the light of the Bat-Signal, he fights crime in the city by night, striking fear in the hearts of evildoers. He protects the innocent, giving them hope that justice will prevail.

He doesn't possess superpowers, but he is highly intelligent and resourceful. He has been called the World's Greatest Detective because there is no villain he cannot track down, no crime he cannot solve, and no scheme so twisted that he cannot untangle. He has mastered several fighting styles and made his body very strong, becoming a formidable opponent for anyone who would dare to face him.

In his constant crusade against crime, Batman has armed himself with the most advanced high-tech equipment, including the amazing rocket-powered car, the Batmobile.

He has also assembled and trained a team of allies, such as Robin and Batgirl. Together, they fight villains as different and deadly as the crime boss Penguin, the eco-terrorist Poison Ivy, and, perhaps Batman's greatest foe, the insane Joker.

As the Dark Knight, he stands against any and all threats to his city, and he always prevails in his battle against evil.

Becoming Batman

The Wayne family had been prominent citizens of Gotham City for several generations. Over the years, the family business, Wayne Enterprises, became a billion-dollar company with interests in shipping, technology, defense, and other money-making ventures around the globe. While most family members were content to help run the business, one heir to the fortune, Thomas Wayne, decided to devote his life to helping others. He wanted to do more than just make money—he wanted to make the world a better place.

Thomas and his wife, Martha, had a son named Bruce. Being a Wayne, the boy had the very best that life had to offer and parents who loved him. Until he was about eight years old, Bruce Wayne was possibly the happiest boy in Gotham City.

Then one evening, Thomas Wayne took Bruce and Martha downtown to watch a movie. Outside the theater, a mugger stepped from the shadows and demanded their valuables. The thief's gun fired twice as he tried to grab Martha's pearl necklace. The boy watched in horror as his dying parents crumpled to the ground.

In that one dark moment, Bruce Wayne's parents were taken away from him and his life was changed forever.

Bruce wanted to save others from the horror that he had faced. However, he wanted to do more than just fight crime and injustice, and he vowed to fight the evil engulfing Gotham City. To do that, he realized he would have to train his mind and body to the peak of perfection. He would become a weapon against the things he hated.

Deciding to leave his pampered life of wealth and privilege behind, he sought out the people who could teach him. In the Himalayan

Mountains, he studied martial arts with the warrior monk Shihan Matsuda, which taught him superior fighting skills and strict control of his body. Another mentor, the brilliant engineer Sergei Alexandrov, helped Bruce master several scientific disciplines.

When Matsuda was killed, it made Bruce even more determined to continue on the path he had chosen. For several years, he traveled across the world mastering gymnastics, detective skills, disguise, and any other talents that would help him in his coming war against the gathering forces of darkness.

After years of intense training, Bruce Wayne returned to Gotham City. He felt ready, but his first attempts at fighting crime left him bruised and battered. Bruce quickly realized that he would have to be more than just a man to truly strike fear into the hearts of the city's evildoers—especially the new and frightening breed of criminals, such as the Red Hood Gang.

One night, while recovering from an unsuccessful fight against that gang, Bruce stumbled into his father's study, where he discovered a hologram that projected a terrifying image of screeching, swarming bats. Bruce realized that the bat was the symbol he needed to tackle the city's corruption and villainy.

He created a suit with a bat-like cape and cowl to conceal his identity. When he leapt from the shadows, the suit created the impression of a dark, monstrous bat. As he hoped, rumors quickly spread in the superstitious underworld that a creature of the night was preying on the wicked. They began to be afraid, and what they feared, they called…
Batman.

NEWS FLASH!

BAT ATTACK!

Report by
VICKI VALE

For quite some time, the mean streets of Gotham City have been no place for ordinary citizens to walk safely at night. However, are things about to get better... or a lot worse?

The *Gazette* spoke to Walter Rubinstein, a longtime Gotham City resident who was minding his own business yesterday, when he witnessed something amazing. "Three kids were robbing an apartment, as bold as you'd like," said Mr. Rubinstein. "I was about to call the police, when suddenly this figure appeared out of nowhere. Here's the crazy thing—he was dressed like some sort of bat! Three against one, but this guy beat them all. Shame he couldn't save the TV they'd nabbed from getting smashed."

So it seems our fair city may have a new resident—a "Batman." However, is he a force for good or evil? Only time will tell.

Personality and abilities

Bruce Wayne was born with a genius-level intellect, but it was his parents' brutal murder that gave him the focus to become an expert in the many disciplines he would need to become Batman. His desire to protect the innocent and see

the wicked punished has given him a strong sense of purpose and a will to succeed that borders on superhuman.

Bruce honed his brilliant mind during four years at college, where he studied a range of subjects, including mathematics, chemistry, computer science, engineering, forensics, and law. By applying this vast knowledge, he is able to outthink his foes and defeat them.

When he needs to stake out places where Batman or Bruce Wayne would be noticed, he uses his skills as a master of disguise. He often poses as the gangster Matches Malone to infiltrate criminal organizations and gain valuable information while undercover.

Batman is regarded as the World's Greatest Detective. A combination of intelligence and intuition allows him to recognize patterns, solve intricate problems and predict villains' moves. Only a few, such as the devious Rā's al Ghūl or the chaotic-minded Joker have managed to outmaneuver him, at least in the short term.

Batman's photographic memory allows him to recall everything he sees with absolute clarity. He makes observations, finds clues that others overlook, and goes over details repeatedly in his mind until the answers to his questions fall into place.

To aid his crime fighting, Batman uses the resources available to him through Wayne Enterprises to furnish his secret lair with the most advanced computers and the best laboratory equipment. His computers are linked to every law enforcement agency in the world, meaning that he can keep track of criminals no matter where they lurk.

Batman has perfected his body, just as he has perfected his mind. A regime of intense exercise, strict diet, and combat practice keep him at the very pinnacle of physical development equal to—if not surpassing—that of an Olympic athlete.

Batman is able to lift more than 1000lb (453.6kg). He can scale the sides of buildings, and has the agility to leap from rooftop to rooftop with ease. His impressive reflexes are lightning quick, he can run

30mph (48.3kph), and he can hold his breath underwater for almost four minutes.

Although the Dark Knight will use all his abilities, and every weapon at his disposal, to subdue an enemy, he will never kill.

He often combines many fighting
techniques at once so that his foe can't
predict his actions. He also uses several types
of weapons such as swords, blades, and
batons, but never a gun.

Batman knows that he has to be in peak
condition—mentally and physically—to face
any enemy that menaces Gotham City.

Armed and dangerous

Batman's suit does much
more than just create the image
of a large bat to scare his enemies.
Like everything in his arsenal, the Batsuit
has many functions. Most importantly, the
cowl protects his secret identity. However, it
also contains communication equipment,
high-tech devices that enhance hearing and
vision, and filters to screen out toxic gases.

The suit itself is made of titanium and
Kevlar weave. It protects Batman's body

from injury by bullets,
punches, and fire.
His armbands have
retractable blades for
defense, and his cape
can be used as a
glider—handy when
patrolling high
above the streets of
Gotham City.

Batman has also created other specialized suits to be used in different environments. One version is designed for high-altitude missions, while another is used underwater, and he even has a stealth suit that makes him invisible! Thermal versions of the Batsuit allow him to fight super-cold villains like Mr. Freeze or hot-tempered criminals who can produce incredible heat, such as Firefly.

Batman continually updates his suits with the most advanced technology available, to ensure that he always stays one step ahead of his enemies.

Batman must be ready for any
situation when he goes on patrol,
whether it's searching the scene of
a crime for clues, or fending off an
archenemy. He wears a Utility Belt packed
with all the gear he needs, including his
Batarangs—sharp bat-shaped blades that
Batman can throw with amazing accuracy.

The Batarangs can be upgraded to emit sonic blasts or knockout gas—or can even explode! Batman also carries a grappling hook and rope for scaling walls, and lock picks for getting through locked doors.

Other important items in his Utility Belt include forensic tools such as a fingerprint kit for analyzing clues, surveillance equipment like cameras and listening devices, and titanium steel handcuffs to restrain the bad guys. Also, because villains like the Scarecrow and the Joker are often armed with toxic weapons or dangerous gases, Batman keeps plenty of medical supplies on hand to heal himself and others caught up in a conflict.

UTILITY BELT

Batman's Utility Belt enhances his abilities and improves his odds of winning a fight. Because he doesn't have superpowers, he must use cunning and technology to defeat villains. The Utility Belt has been a major part of Batman's arsenal, and its contents are always changing.

ADDITIONAL ITEMS

- A breathing mask, in case Batman is trapped at a location where air has been poisoned.

- A cutting tool, to slice through rope or anything that is being used to bind Batman.

- A fingerprint kit, ideal when he has to identify someone and he's not near the Batcave.

- Plastic explosives, which can blow up locked doors and walls.

- Toxins, powerful enough to knock out his strongest foes.

BATARANGS

These razor-sharp weapons are thrown with perfect precision by Batman.

COMMUNICATOR

A smart computerized device that can even make holographic recordings.

MINIATURE CAMERA

This digital camera also has a flash that can temporarily blind attackers!

GRAPPLING HOOK

Useful for scaling high walls and quick escapes.

However, even Batman can't carry everything in his Utility Belt. He also uses several vehicles for crime fighting—the most important being the Batmobile.

Whenever the Bat-Signal shines above Gotham City, the Dark Knight races to the scene in his rocket-powered Batmobile. Like all of his equipment, the Batmobile has been modified several times over the years. It has evolved into a combination of high-speed performance racer, urban assault vehicle, and mobile crime-fighting lab.

The Batmobile is incredibly fast and maneuverable even though it is so heavily shielded it can withstand armor-piercing shells. It also carries additional medical equipment, and its advanced on-board computer system is linked to Batman's powerful mainframe computer. This allows Batman to control the Batmobile remotely, meaning it can come to him wherever he needs it. The Batmobile is also armed with nonlethal offensive weapons, such as tear gas emitters, smoke-screen grenades, tire-piercing spikes, and super adhesive sprays.

BEYOND THE BATMOBILE

The Batmobile isn't the Dark Knight's only means of transportation. He has an amazing array of vehicles to get him on the scene—fast!

BATPLANE

The Batplane cost $46million (£30million) to build. When it reaches its cruising altitude of 35,000-45,0000ft (10,670-13,715m), its wings retract. Once it climbs above 55,000ft (16,765m), the Batplane enters stealth mode. Its "smart" paint reacts to the falling air pressure, camouflaging the plane's exterior.

BATCYCLE

When Batman needs a vehicle that is easier to move through crowded Gotham City streets than the Batmobile, he chooses the swift and maneuverable Batcycle. This mighty motorcycle is a modified street bike.

BAT-GLIDER

Not to be confused with the Batplane, this impressive device is designed to resemble a bat's wingspan and gives Batman the ability to fly. He hides various Bat-gliders around Gotham City.

BATBOAT

Batman's sleek watercraft is needed when he has to pursue criminals in Gotham City's river. The Batboat can reach up to 120mph (193kph) and can even travel underwater if required.

Locations

Its history is centuries old, but Gotham City truly took shape when Alan Wayne, Bruce Wayne's great-grandfather, funded its transformation into a modern metropolis.

Already a thriving port, Gotham City quickly grew into a mighty megacity—thanks largely to the Wayne family's enterprising spirit. But in the shadow of progress and wealth, crime and corruption soon spread through its streets.

Gotham City quickly became a breeding ground for mobsters, thieves and lowlifes. It also began to attract uncanny criminals such as the menacing metahuman Poison Ivy, and the Joker, a vile villain bent on creating malicious mayhem for a laugh.

Thankfully, Gotham City also has its share of heroes. Batman has inspired others, such as Commissioner Gordon, Robin, Batgirl, and even the good people of Gotham City to fight the growing evil that threatens their great city.

As heir to Wayne Enterprises, one of the world's largest multinational companies, Bruce Wayne pretends to be a billionaire playboy only interested in fast cars, parties, and spending money. That way no one suspects he is really Batman.

He makes his home at Wayne Manor, the grand estate where the Wayne family has lived for many generations. But like its owner, Wayne Manor harbors a secret—the Batcave! In the hidden caverns beneath the estate, Bruce has put his company's vast resources to good use. He has unrestricted access to all the computer electronics, chemical manufacturing, aeronautic equipment, robotics, and more to outfit his underground hideout with advanced technology and crime-fighting gear.

The Batcave contains a crime lab, engineering workshops, and a gym, as well as full medical facilities that can treat anything from broken bones to chemical exposure. However, Batman's greatest tool in his fight against crime is his Batcomputer, which allows him to keep an eye on everything happening in Gotham City, and gather information from around the world.

SECRETS OF THE BATCAVE

The Batcave contains a state-of-the-art crime lab, equipment workshops, a library, a gym, medical facilities, and the coolest garage in Gotham City!

1. TYRANNOSAURUS REX

Although he looks like he could go on the rampage at any moment, this mechanical Tyrannosaurus Rex is a trophy from Batman's adventure on Dinosaur Island. Batman likes a keepsake from every enemy he defeats!

2. VEHICLES

There is plenty of parking for the Batmobile, Batcycle, and even Bruce's Lamborghini sports car. The Batcave also has a hangar and dock.

3. LABS

The cave contains a fully-equipped crime lab as well as workshops to maintain Batman's amazing armor, weaponry, and vehicles. There is also a gym with up-to-the-minute training equipment to help the Dark Knight stay in peak condition.

4. SECRET IDENTITY

The key to keeping Bruce Wayne's identity a secret is his Batsuit. The cave holds the various special suits he needs, as well as outfits for teammates, like Robin.

5. SECRET ENTRANCE

The Batcave can be reached using a variety of secret entrances. There are doors behind a clock and bookcase in Wayne Manor, a hidden passageway beneath Bruce Wayne's chair in Wayne Enterprises, and a tunnel for the Batmobile concealed by a hologram.

6. COMPUTERS

The Batcave boasts the latest technology so Batman can monitor crisis points anywhere. His satellite-linked Batcomputer gathers and stores all the data he requires to stay ahead of his enemies.

Arkham Asylum is a high-security psychiatric hospital on the edge of Gotham City. The hospital is home to some of the most notorious criminals that Batman has ever fought. Villains deemed to be too psychotic and violent for regular prisons like Blackgate are sent to Arkham. The Joker, the Riddler, and the Scarecrow have all been inmates at various times. Arkham also holds sane but dangerous villains who require special conditions to keep them under lock and key, such as the frosty Mr. Freeze and the toxic Poison Ivy. However, despite Arkham's many high-tech security measures, these crafty criminals often manage to escape.

Since it first opened, Arkham has badly affected many of the people connected to it. Amadeus Arkham, its founder, went insane and became a patient in his own hospital. His descendant, Jeremiah Arkham, was head psychiatrist until he became the villain Black Mask. The Joker's therapist became the crazy criminal Harley Quinn.

Arkham Asylum had to be rebuilt after the brutal warrior Bane led a large prison break by the inmates. The new institution is still as foreboding as the madmen it houses.

INSIDE THE MADHOUSE!

Over the years, many of Batman's most dangerous enemies have been imprisoned within Arkham Asylum's walls. Even the asylum's founder, Amadeus Arkham, was driven insane. Dare you venture inside?

Main catwalk to central tower

In a ploy to lure Batman into a trap, the Joker took over Arkham Asylum and freed several of its inmates, including Maxie Zeus and the Mad Hatter.

Heavy equipment outer doors

After Batman disappeared a few years ago and was presumed dead, Black Mask seized his chance and released the prisoners from Arkham Asylum, declaring himself their new leader.

A group of Batman's deadliest enemies, including Two-Face, the Scarecrow, and Killer Croc, once joined forces to break out of Arkham Asylum. Batman was forced to team up with the Joker to stop them.

Outer wall: 30in (76.2cm) reinforced concrete. Windows: super-strong plastic

Maximum security containment cells

Violent ward

gh-security risk cells

When Arkham Asylum was destroyed in an explosion caused by the angel of vengeance, The Spectre, Bruce Wayne gave Wayne Manor to Gotham City. It briefly became a home for the criminally insane and changed its name to Arkham Manor.

Multi-level security:
• Video surveillance of 86% of entire facility; 100% of exterior
• Motion detectors throughout
• Electronic pass system

Main security command center

Internal high-security doors: transparent, super-strong plastic

After a murder occurred at Arkham Manor, Batman went undercover as Jack Shaw to find the killer. Batman had to live among some of his deadliest foes like Mr. Freeze and Victor Zsasz to uncover the truth. The killer turned out to be a former laborer who went mad inside Arkham.

Fearsome foes

Batman has many enemies, but none compare to the Joker. This sinister clown is a comic genius at causing chaos in Gotham City. No one—not even Batman— is really sure of the Joker's true origin. Many think that he was once a member of the Red Hood Gang who fell into a vat of chemicals when he was chased by Batman through an old factory. The young man emerged from the blistering bath with his skin bleached white, his hair turned green, and his mind twisted beyond repair!

Despite his madness, the Joker exhibits an amazing talent for chemistry and engineering. He has created an extremely lethal arsenal of acids, joy buzzers, and novelty gags that no one finds funny. "Joker venom" is his most diabolical concoction. Small doses can put people under his control, while larger doses can make them literally die laughing with gruesome smiles on their faces.

Over the years, he has masterminded many terrible plots against his archenemy Batman. At first, he only wanted to eliminate the Dark Knight, but now he gets more sadistic glee out of kidnapping and threatening those closest to Batman, like Robin, Batgirl, and other allies, with horrible deaths.

While treating the Joker at Arkham Asylum, Dr. Harleen Quinzel became hopelessly fascinated by the madman. When her own mind finally snapped, she took the name Harley Quinn and became the criminal clown's accomplice. Harley Quinn is willing to go along with the Joker's schemes no matter how insane. However, she is more than just a sidekick. She is just as capable of cruelty as the Joker, and loves making mischief and mayhem of her own.

Harley Quinn is extremely acrobatic, and her madcap fighting style makes her a tricky opponent in hand-to-hand combat. She has successfully fought Batman and other heroes who can never be sure what move she is going to make next. Her current weapon of choice is an oversized mallet, but she's also very handy with her trusty pop gun.

She has been known to team up with Poison Ivy and Catwoman. However, like the Joker, Harley Quinn is too unstable to be trusted. Her alliances usually fall apart when she almost always veers away from the plan to follow her own wild impulses—often leaving her partners in the lurch!

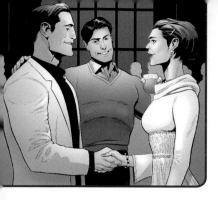

District Attorney Harvey Dent was a beacon of light to the law-abiding citizens of Gotham City. For a time, he even became Batman's ally in his war on corruption in the city. Dent worked hard to put criminals behind bars, but despite his noble efforts, he was sometimes willing to go outside the law to get results. This darker side of his personality would one day overwhelm him when the mob horribly disfigured half of his face with acid and killed his wife.

Driven insane, Dent became Two-Face, a criminal with a split personality—rational one moment and monstrous the next. He came to believe that order or chaos should be decided with a toss of his scarred coin: heads you live, tails you die! Over the years, he has come into conflict with Batman as he plotted to gain control of Gotham City's underworld. He has occasionally forged alarming alliances with equally unpredictable villains like the Joker and Scarecrow, only to be thwarted by Batman or his own dual nature.

Batman continues to hope that he can one day help Dent, but is the Dark Knight merely a coin toss away from defeat?

Oswald Cobblepot was forever picked on as a boy because of his short stature and physical deformities, which gave him a birdlike appearance. The experience also gave him a fierce will to win and the ability to really hold a grudge. Nicknamed the Penguin, Cobblepot quickly proved himself to be smart and savage. By successfully working his way up in society through illegal activities, the Penguin became one of the leading figures in Gotham City's underworld. His actions eventually brought him into direct conflict with Batman, leading to many setbacks in his criminal fortunes.

Despite his dumpy demeanor, the Penguin is a very capable fighter, able to

go toe-to-toe with the Dark Knight. He also carries umbrellas armed with deadly surprises. Most models contain a razor-sharp sword hidden in the shaft that he can pull from the handle. Others release knockout gas to stun his foes, while another model is a camouflaged machine gun.

Opponents underestimate the Penguin at their own peril. He once made himself Mayor of Gotham City, and set the inmates of Arkham Asylum and Blackgate Prison against each other, until the Dark Knight removed him from office. Yet, try as he might, Batman can never keep this bad bird caged for long.

Much like the Penguin, Pamela Isley had a very troubled childhood. A rare, sensitive skin condition kept her at home, and having few friends to play with, she would spend her time in her family's shady garden, where her fascination with plant life took root. Years later, her knowledge of plant biology landed her a job at Wayne Enterprises in its bio-chemical division, but an accident with one of her experiments granted her the power to control plants and made her immune to all poisons, venoms, and even nasty viruses.

Taking the name Poison Ivy, she mostly enjoys being bad, though often in a very rash attempt to protect the environment. She once tricked the villain Clayface into attacking the Penguin's polluting factories, but her plan drew her into direct combat against Batman.

On her good days, she has teamed up with some of Batman's allies and even helped the Dark Knight gain immunity to the lethal Fear Toxin, created by the sinister Scarecrow. With Ivy's help, Batman was able to save all of Gotham City from being poisoned. However, no matter what hint of goodness may bloom in her, Poison Ivy's more wicked ways always sprout, causing trouble to grow.

Having discovered the secret of near immortality, Rā's al Ghūl has mastered many fighting styles and acquired more skills and knowledge than anyone could learn in a single lifetime. As such, it makes him one of Batman's toughest opponents. More than six hundred years ago, Rā's discovered the fabled Lazarus Pits. By bathing in the Pits, his youth and vitality would be restored, and even deadly wounds could be healed.

He founded the League of Assassins to fight corruption, but by the 21st century, the League itself had become evil as Rā's slowly lost his sanity through continual use of the Lazarus Pits.

Having fought the League and many of Rā's al Ghūl's allies, Batman eventually came face to face with

Rā's when the ageless fiend tried to unleash
a lethal virus on the world. They have clashed
several times since, with Batman's intellect
and tenacity always defeating Rā's, and even
earning him the immortal's respect.

Despite their intense rivalry, their lives
became strangely entangled when Rā's al
Ghūl's daughter, Talia, gave birth to Batman's
son, Damian. The boy has often been caught
in the middle of his grandfather's intricate
and unending plots against his father!

Born in a brutal prison, Bane was raised in violence and quickly learned how to fight to survive. He grew into a man of immense size and muscle, who also showed savage intelligence, tactical genius, martial arts mastery, and, above all, iron-willed ambition. At some point during his life in prison, he was given a dangerous drug called Venom. It greatly enhanced his already prodigious strength, speed, and endurance to superhuman levels. With his newfound abilities, he finally escaped.

Bane headed to Gotham City, to take over the city's criminal gangs. As he made his plans, Bane studied Gotham City's protector, Batman, deducing that he was really Bruce Wayne. Bane ambushed Batman, breaking his back and leaving him for dead. However, Batman bounced back and eventually defeated Bane.

Over the years, Bane has proven to be one of the Dark Knight's deadliest adversaries. Unlike madmen such as the Joker, Bane and Batman acknowledge the noble qualities they share, like two brave fighters who know that a rematch is inevitable.

The secret society known as the Court of Owls has ruled Gotham City for hundreds of years. The members come from some of Gotham City's oldest and wealthiest families, who use power, money, and even murder to get their way.

Working silently from the shadows, their most terrifying weapons are their assassins known as the Talons. The Owls take young people, often circus performers who exhibit skills such as acrobatics and knife throwing, and train them to become ruthless enforcers of the court's judgments. They have even found a way to bring Talons back from the dead, making them seem frighteningly unstoppable! At one time, the Owls considered a young acrobat named Dick Grayson as a candidate for a Talon, but were thwarted when Bruce Wayne took the boy under his wing.

Their attempt to murder Bruce Wayne led them into open conflict with Batman and his allies. This led to the Owls being exposed, several of their Talons turning on them, and their organization falling into disarray. However, the Court of Owls is far from finished, and it continues to seek a verdict of death against the Dark Knight!

Deeply troubled by the tests of terror that his father put him through as a child, Jonathan Crane grew up wanting to control fear.

He slowly slid into a life of crime, becoming determined to spread dread and terror across Gotham City. He developed a Fear Toxin that could create horrifying hallucinations in his victims, and he wore a ragged mask and costume to become the Scarecrow.

Always able to conquer his fears, the Dark Knight has successfully defeated the Scarecrow many times. This gave the villain the ingenious idea of creating the vision of a peaceful Gotham City in the minds of Batman and his allies to make them forget about fighting crime. For a while the plan worked, but

the Dark Knight eventually saw through the delusion and brought the Scarecrow's dream of a Batman-free Gotham City to an end.

Despite this, Batman knows that the Scarecrow is always lurking in the shadows determined to give him a fatal fright!

Obsessed with riddles, wordplay, and intricate puzzles, young Edward Nygma grew up smugly thinking that he was smarter than most people around him. Clever and ambitious, he was eventually employed in an important position at Wayne Enterprises.

When Bruce Wayne returned from his travels to take over the company, a jealous Nygma hired the Red Hood Gang to kill Bruce. The plan failed, but it led Nygma to embrace a life of crime and take on a new persona as the Riddler.

His schemes grew ever more outlandish and at

one point he was able to turn Gotham City into an overgrown jungle with a chemical developed by Poison Ivy. He set himself up as the king of this savage jungle, but in the survival of the fittest, he was no match for Batman.

While imprisoned in Arkham Asylum, he proved to his fellow inmate, the Joker, that he was a master of strategy and escape, joining the insane clown in his latest fiendish escapade. Although he's not nearly as psychotic as the Joker, Batman never underrates the Riddler, who always has a deadly question mark hanging over his head.

Basil Karlo wanted to be a famous actor, but he wasn't very talented. He agreed to work for the Penguin in exchange for a magic clay that the Penguin claimed could help his acting career. The substance entered his body, and Karlo developed the ability to alter his appearance— he could look like anyone he wanted. At first this helped him land better roles, but soon there were bad side effects that turned him into a violent, walking hunk of living clay.

Enjoying the criminal activities he performed for Penguin, Karlo embraced his new life as Clayface. He could imitate anyone, he had

great strength, and his flexible body let him
slip through tight spaces as well as absorb
punches and bullets. In the hopes of getting
rich quickly, he tried to impersonate billionaire
Bruce Wayne, not knowing he was Batman.
In the inevitable conflict, the Dark Knight
trapped Clayface in a special container,
but the villain was able to slip through the
hands of the authorities. Now Batman can
never be sure whose face Clayface will be
wearing when they next meet.

Victor Fries had devoted his life to studying cryogenics and keeping things alive at sub-zero temperatures.

While working for Wayne Enterprises, Fries became obsessed with a cryogenically frozen woman named Nora. He fell in love with Nora and even began to believe that she was his wife. A lab accident doused Fries with experimental chemicals that turned him icy cold, forcing him to wear a special suit of armor that would allow him to survive in the normal temperature of the outside world.

Building a freeze gun, Fries set out on a criminal spree across Gotham City as Mr. Freeze.

He wanted to steal enough money to enable him to continue his research and reclaim Nora, with the desperate hope of one day being able to revive her.

In addition to his own highly warped scientific schemes, he has teamed up with Batman's enemies on several occasions. However, no matter what his plans, this ice-cold criminal always gets put back in deep freeze by the Dark Knight.

Waylon Jones was born with a horrific genetic mutation that made him look like a large human crocodile. He has tough, scaly skin that can deflect bullets and hard blows. His sharp claws can tear through wood and concrete just as easily as they can his opponents. He is savagely strong and fast, despite his huge size. This has all earned him the feared name Killer Croc.

Bullied his whole life because of his strange looks, he became a ferocious fighter and a criminal to survive. He also protects the homeless and the helpless who are forced to live in the sewers below Gotham City. He has sided with villains such as Scarecrow against Batman, but mostly to defend his subterranean kingdom of outcasts. He once was beaten by the mighty Bane in combat, and has acted as a bodyguard for Selina Kyle, aka Catwoman. Still, Batman knows that the cold-blooded killer in Croc is waiting to surface and will one day snap!

Dr. Kirk Langstrom was searching for a way to help deaf and blind children, but the formula that he discovered had unforeseen and hideous side effects. Langstrom developed the features of a bat. He grew fur, sharp claws, and fangs. He could fly with leathery wings, and his long ears gave him the power of echolocation: He could use sound to "see" in the dark.

He had become the Man-Bat!

At first, Langstrom was Batman's ally, but later the Dark Knight suspected that his Man-Bat side was growing much wilder. He worried that Man-Bat had committed a series of gruesome murders that he couldn't remember. Langstrom soon realized that his wife Francine had also used a version of the formula on herself—one that contained the DNA of a vampire bat. He had not committed the murders; she had! Not only that, she liked being a bat creature, and even called herself the Bat-Queen.

Man-Bat would eventually turn bad and team up with the Dark Knight's enemies, but Batman still hopes that he can find a cure for this scientist-turned-monster.

BATMAN'S GREATEST BATTLES!

Batman has been protecting Gotham City for years, but some villains just don't know when to quit. Here are some of the Dark Knight's toughest fights.

During one battle, **Bane** enhanced his strength with a new version of the drug, Venom. Just as Bane was about to hurl Batman over a cliff, the Dark Knight made his foe swallow a Venom antidote. With Bane in a weakened state, Batman managed to push him into the sea.

The **Joker** is one of the few villains who has come close to defeating Batman. He once took advantage of an impaired Batman to release a poison into the air that turned its victims into copies of the Joker. Batman was even imprisoned in Arkham Asylum and, once freed, he was forced to turn to the evil Court of Owls for help in bringing down the Joker.

Rā's al Ghūl, one of Batman's greatest foes, has tried to kill him on countless occasions. When the Dark Knight first encountered the powerful villain, Ghūl challenged him to a spectacular sword fight, which Batman ultimately won.

The **Scarecrow** has clashed with the Dark Knight many times. On one occasion, he managed to kidnap Batman and infect him with a Fear Toxin. With Superman's help, Batman fought off the toxin's effects and he subdued the Scarecrow.

The Court of Owls' assassins, the **Talons**, once captured Batman and placed him in their malicious maze. The Talons tried everything to break the Dark Knight's spirit, but when he saw a picture of Alan Wayne, an ancestor killed by the Talons, he found the strength to win.

The **Riddler** took over Gotham City for a whole year, forcing Bruce Wayne to go underground. The Riddler was stopped thanks to Batman's cunning and help from some of his closest allies, including James Gordon—a police sergeant at the time.

Awesome allies

Batman has many allies in his war against crime and evil. None is more trusted than Alfred Pennyworth. Alfred has been the butler at Wayne Manor for many years, and raised Bruce after his parents were murdered.

Alfred's duties run far beyond those of any normal butler. In addition to making sure that everything at Wayne Manor runs smoothly, he helps Bruce Wayne keep up his image as a billionaire playboy. He also maintains Batman's suits, the Batmobile, and all the workings of the Batcave, in readiness for the Dark Knight's next mission.

Having served in the military, he has fighting and medical experience as well.

From the Batcomputer, Alfred is able to provide valuable information to Batman while he is out on patrol. He also attends to Batman's wounds in the Batcave's high-tech medical facility.

Even though Alfred is often critical of the serious risks taken by Batman, he is fiercely loyal and dependable. He has also helped several of Batman's friends, especially his young protégés, like Robin.

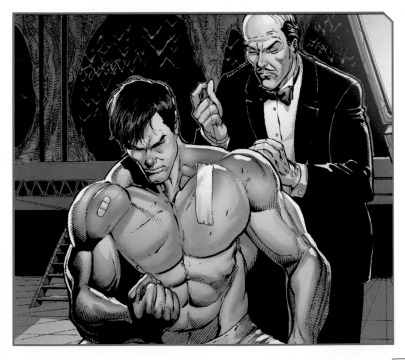

Robin fights alongside Batman, and several people have assumed that vital role over the years, becoming heroes in their own right. Batman has taken these young apprentices under his wing to train them and help them focus their talent and energy into helping him rid Gotham City of crime.

No Robin is dearer to Batman than Damian Wayne, his son. His mother is Talia al Ghūl, the daughter of Rā's al Ghūl—one of the world's greatest villains! Despite this, after Damian met his father, he chose to fight on the side of good. Fatally wounded in a vicious battle with The Heretic, Damian was restored to life by Batman using alien technology. As father and son, they share an unbreakable bond in their quest for justice.

THE MANY FACES OF ROBIN

Batman often works with a younger ally, Robin, to keep the streets of Gotham City safe. There have been four boys who have adopted this role. The first was Dick Grayson, followed by Jason Todd and Tim Drake. The newest Robin is Bruce Wayne's own son, Damian.

JASON TODD
Batman first met Jason Todd when the street criminal tried to steal the Batmobile's tires. Batman placed him in a school for youngsters in trouble with the law, before making him the second Robin. Jason now fights crime as the Red Hood and is prepared to use lethal force.

DICK GRAYSON
Orphaned when his acrobat parents were killed, Dick Grayson was adopted by Bruce Wayne who taught him to use his skills to combat crime. Many years later he became the costumed hero Nightwing, and now operates undercover as Agent 37.

TIM DRAKE

After watching Dick Grayson in action at the circus, Tim Drake worked out the secret identities of Batman and Robin. He followed their adventures and when the two super heroes were captured, he became Robin to rescue them! He has also changed his crime-fighting identity, and now battles evil as the Red Robin.

DAMIAN WAYNE

The latest Robin is the son of Bruce Wayne and Talia al Ghūl, the daughter of one of Batman's most dangerous foes, Rā's al Ghūl. Damian died during a fierce fight, but was brought back to life soon afterwards, with short-lived superpowers.

Super heroes aren't the only people in Gotham City fighting crime. James Gordon is the commissioner of the Gotham City Police Department (G.C.P.D.) and Batman's ally. Gordon shines the Bat-Signal in the sky to let Batman know he's needed.

Many people question why their police commissioner works with a vigilante. However, Gordon knows what might happen if Batman was not around to protect the city against the likes of the Joker, the Scarecrow, and even the police force itself!

The Gotham City Police Department has been troubled by corruption for many years. G.C.P.D. members, from uniformed officers to high-ranking officials, have been linked to criminal activity. However, there are still some honest cops on the force, like the gruff Harvey Bullock, and his whip-smart partner, Renee Montoya. Both back Commissioner Gordon's association with Batman. Yet they all fear that if the Dark Knight steps too far outside the law, they'll have no choice but to bring him to justice.

Selina Kyle is the orphaned daughter of a Gotham City crime boss. At an early age she became a thief and cat burglar—talents that she excelled at. Selina later adopted the identity of Catwoman, and her successful criminal career brought her to the attention of Batman.

Armed with sharp claws on her gloves and a whip that she wields with great skill, Catwoman is an impressive opponent. While not superhuman, her agility, speed, reflexes, and stealth border on being genuinely feline. Her abilities as a thief to scale walls, slip into small spaces, and get past any form of security are second to none. Added to that, she has been trained in multiple forms of hand-to-hand combat, making her an accomplished and fearsome fighter. She has fought Batman on several occasions and has often come out on top.

Over time, Catwoman has changed her criminal ways, and she now fights on the side of good—though it is always on her own terms. She and Batman have become allies and even share romantic feelings for each other. However, their crusade to make Gotham City a safer place for its citizens always comes first.

Batman has had several young allies who have worn the Robin costume, before his son, Damian, took on the role. Tim Drake was a superb detective. Jason Todd's dark personality made him the most driven. However, the very first Robin was Dick Grayson.

Dick grew up as a circus acrobat, but a mobster killed his parents, leaving him an orphan. Bruce Wayne took the boy into his care and revealed to him that he was Batman. Building on Dick's acrobatic abilities, Bruce trained him to be a fellow crusader, helping

him become adept at using weapons such as batons and staffs.

When he was older, Dick parted ways with Batman and set out on his own, becoming the hero Nightwing. Occasionally, he has returned to help his mentor—sometimes even becoming Batman when Bruce Wayne was injured—and has come to the aid of other members of the crime-fighting Batman family. At Batman's request, Dick has gone undercover to infiltrate the mysterious criminal organization called Spyral, where he is known as Agent 37.

Commissioner Gordon's daughter, Barbara, grew up wanting to be a super hero. Incredibly smart and athletic, she came to the attention of Batman. Barbara trained with the Dark Knight and was soon fighting alongside him and Robin as Batgirl. Tragedy struck when she was shot and paralyzed by the Joker, ending her crime-fighting career for a short time.

With a combination of rigorous training, innovative surgery, and steely determination

she fully recovered and returned to battle crime. Her many talents include a genius intellect, a flawless memory and a mastery of many forms of martial arts, including judo and kickboxing. She is also great at wielding a baton, and can throw Batarangs with pinpoint precision. Best of all, Batgirl is a highly skilled computer engineer and hacker—even more so than Batman! She once created a computer virus to wipe clean the information from a villain's mind. She has also lent her extensive skills to the all-female super hero team, the Birds of Prey, helping them to clean up Gotham City.

ARE YOU READY TO JOIN THE BATMAN FAMILY?

The Dark Knight often teams up with other heroes to keep Gotham City safe. Take this quiz to find out which ally's talents you share the most—and learn about other members of the Batman family.

1. **You're about to patrol the streets of Gotham City. What's the most important thing you'll need?**

a. Dark clothes, so you're not seen by any villains ★

b. As much technology as your Utility Belt can carry ●

c. A couple of flares to help get you out of a tough spot ◆

d. Just your skill and instincts ♥

2. **You've spotted a possible crime taking place. What do you do first?**

a. Take out your radar scanner and check how many villains are up ahead ●

b. Sneak a bit closer to assess the situation ★

c. Leap straight into the action—you can handle it ♥

d. Create a diversion to distract most of the bad guys ◆

3. **Batman has asked you along on a mission. How do you help out?**

a. Fight right alongside him. Wherever he goes, you go ♥

b. Rescue him the moment it looks like he's about to be defeated ◆

c. Check out the area before Batman arrives to find all potential threats ★

d. Update his Utility Belt, so that he has the most suitable gear ●

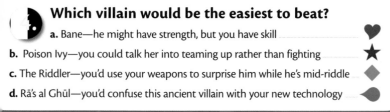

Which villain would be the easiest to beat?

a. Bane—he might have strength, but you have skill

b. Poison Ivy—you could talk her into teaming up rather than fighting

c. The Riddler—you'd use your weapons to surprise him while he's mid-riddle

d. Rā's al Ghūl—you'd confuse this ancient villain with your new technology

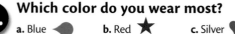

5. Which color do you wear most?

a. Blue   **b.** Red   **c.** Silver   **d.** Orange

BATWOMAN
Highly skilled in hand-to-hand combat, Batwoman's greatest talent is her stealth. Trained by her ex-military father, her secret identity is Kate Kane, and she has become a real force to be reckoned with.

BATWING
Batwing is Luke Fox, the son of Bruce Wayne's friend and boss of Wayne Enterprises, Lucius Fox. Luke is great at martial arts and uses a special Batsuit so he can fly over Gotham City on the lookout for crime.

BLUEBIRD
Bluebird, aka Harper Row, grew up in the Narrows of Gotham City with her younger brother. Bluebird is a genius with electronics and, after a tough upbringing, she can deal with any situation that is thrown at her.

HAWKFIRE
Hawkfire is Batwoman's cousin, Bette Kane. She is a superb gymnast and kickboxer, and is kitted out with retractable wings, flares, and a wrist-mounted flamethrower—some villains find her too hot to handle!

The Justice League is a group of super heroes who band together to defend Earth from dangers greater than any one of them could face alone. The team began when Batman partnered with the power ring–wearing Green Lantern to fight the demonic Darkseid. Knowing that Superman was the mightiest being on the planet, they enlisted his help and the Justice League was born.

Soon, other heroes joined, including the Amazon warrior, Wonder Woman; The Fastest Man Alive, The Flash; the half-man, half-machine, Cyborg; and ruler of the underwater kingdom of Atlantis, Aquaman.

Together, they have overcome conquerors from Earth and outer space. They have also faced more sinister threats like the Amazo Virus, created by the villainous Lex Luthor, which gave super powers to ordinary people, turning them evil! When Batman was infected by the virus, the Justice League teamed up with Luthor to save mankind… and their friend.

THE JUSTICE LEAGUE

With so many powerful villains, the world can be a very dangerous place. Luckily, Batman has the Justice League as allies, whom he can call on for help.

SUPERMAN

Born on the doomed planet, Krypton, Superman was sent to Earth as a baby. His real name is Kal-El, but the humans who adopted him named him Clark Kent.

POWERS: Flying, super-strength, super-speed, heat vision, and breath that can freeze anything.

WONDER WOMAN

Born on Paradise Island, also called Themiscyra, Wonder Woman is an Amazonian princess. She is the daughter of Queen Hippolyta and Zeus, king of the Greek gods.

POWERS: Super-strength, flying, indestructible bracelets, and the Lasso of Truth, which forces others to reveal their secrets.

THE FLASH

Barry Allen is a police scientist whose life was changed forever when a lightning bolt struck his lab, causing chemicals to spill over him.

POWERS: Super-speed, healing, and passing through objects.

CYBORG

Victor Stone was attacked by a creature from an inter-dimensional portal. The only way he could survive was for his father, Silas, to create a cyborg body for him.

POWERS: Super-strength, genius-level intellect, and flying.

GREEN LANTERN

Hal Jordan was a fighter pilot when he met Abin Sur, a dying alien who was part of an intergalactic police force. Hal's fearlessness made him the obvious choice to replace Sur.

POWERS: Uses his power ring to fly and make real whatever he can imagine.

AQUAMAN

Arthur Curry is the son of lighthouse keeper Tom Curry and Atlanna, who came from the underwater kingdom of Atlantis. He gave up the throne of Atlantis to become a super hero.

POWERS: The ability to swim super-fast, enhanced strength, and mind control over sea creatures.

Quiz

1. What terrible incident makes Bruce Wayne determined to fight crime?

2. Who were Bruce Wayne's teachers as he traveled around the world learning how to improve himself?

3. Which criminal does Batman disguise himself as when he goes undercover to get information?

4. Who is Batman's greatest foe?

5. How much can Batman lift?

6. Who is the latest Robin?

7. Batman's bulletproof suit is made out of which materials?

8. What giant mechanical creature is kept in the Batcave as a trophy?

9. How much did the Batplane cost to build?

10. What is Harley Quinn's current weapon of choice?

11. Which feathered court works outside the law to bring down Batman?

12. How does the G.C.P.D.'s Commissioner Gordon contact Batman?

13. Which criminal organization has Dick Grayson infiltrated as Agent 37?

14. What is Batwoman's relationship to Hawkfire?

15. Which all-powerful alien villain first brought the Justice League together to fight him?

See page 95 for answers.

Glossary

Acrobatic
The ability to perform gymnastic feats with great skill.

Alter ego
A person's hidden side or personality.

Arsenal
A collection of weapons.

Assassin
Someone hired to kill.

Camouflage
Hiding something using a disguise.

Concoction
A mixture of different things.

Contingency
An alternate or emergency plan.

Cryogenics
The science of very low temperatures.

Cutting-edge
Very modern, with the latest features.

Deformity
Something disfigured or misshapen.

DNA
A substance that carries the genetic information of plants and animals.

Demeanor
A person's appearance and behavior.

Eco-terrorist
Someone who uses extreme measures to stop damage to the environment.

Echolocation
Using sound and echoes to get around in the dark.

Engulf
To flow over and enclose something.

Foreboding
A feeling something bad will happen.

Forensic
Using scientific methods to solve crime.

Formidable
Possessing immense power or ability.

Gargoyle
A stone creature used on buildings.

Genetic / Genes
Part of a cell that controls the growth and appearance of living things.

Hacker
A person who secretly gains access to a computer system to get at someone else's data.

Hallucinations
Something experienced only in the mind that seems real but is not.

Hologram
A three-dimensional image produced by light.

Immortality
The ability to live forever.

Impaired
Reduced or weakened in strength.

Infiltrate
To join a group to secretly obtain information from them.

Infrared
A type of light that feels warm but cannot be seen.

Innovative
Using new methods or ideas.

Invulnerability
Unable to be harmed.

Inter-dimensional
An imagined dimension or place beyond our own.

Intergalactic
The vast space between galaxies.

Kevlar
Strong, lightweight material used to make items bulletproof.

Lethal
Very dangerous and may cause death.

Malicious
Intending to do harm to someone.

Martial arts
A traditional Asian form of fighting or self-defense, like karate and judo.

Mentor
A trusted and experienced teacher.

Metahuman
Someone with superhuman powers.

Mutation
A genetic change in a plant or animal.

Notorious
Someone or something famous for being bad.

Outlandish
Something that is wild and unusual.

Persona
A person's outward personality.

Psychotic
A mad, insane person.

Prodigious
Something that is amazing, marvelous, or very big.

Protégé
A young person who is taught by someone with a lot of experience.

Prowess
Possessing great ability.

Regime
A regular activity.

Rehabilitate
Restore someone's good health or reputation.

Retractable
To pull something back into something that encloses it.

Subterranean
Located or living underground

Stake out / Surveillance
Carefully watching someone, usually to prevent a crime.

Thermal
The ability of special garments to retain heat.

Toxic
Containing poisonous material.

Titanium
A very strong and flexible metal.

Vigilante
Someone who fights crime outside of the law.

Index

Abin Sur 89
Agent 37 74, 81, 91
Alan Wayne 30, 69
Alfred Pennyworth 70–71
Amadeus Arkham 37
Amazo Virus 86
Amazon 86, 88
Aquaman 86, 89
Arkham Asylum 36–37, 38–39, 42, 47, 59, 68
Arkham Manor 39
Arthur Curry 89 see also Aquaman
Atlantis 86, 89
Bane 37, 52–53, 65, 68, 85
Barbara Gordon 82–83
    see also Batgirl
Barry Allen 89 see also The Flash
Basil Karlo 60 see also Clayface
Bat-glider 29
Bat-Queen 67
Bat-Signal 4, 26, 76
Batarangs 22–23, 24
Batboat 29
Batcave 32–33, 34–35, 70, 90
Batcomputer 33, 35, 71
Batcycle 28, 34
Batgirl 5, 41, 82–83
Batman 4–5, 6, 11–12, 14–29, 31–33, 35–36, 38–47, 49–53, 55–57, 59, 61, 63–83, 86–91
    see also Dark Knight
Batman Family 84–85
Batmobile 4, 26–27, 28, 34, 70, 74
Batplane 28
Batwing 85
Batwoman 85, 91
Bette Kane 85 see also Hawkfire
Birds of Prey 83
Black Mask 37, 38
Blackgate Prison 36, 47
Bluebird 85
Bruce Wayne 7–11, 14–15, 30–35, 54–55, 58, 61, 70, 74–75, 81
    see also Batman, Dark Knight

Catwoman 43, 78–79
Clark Kent 88 see also Superman
Clayface 49, 60–61
Commissioner James Gordon 31, 69, 76–77, 91
Court of Owls 54–55, 69
Cyborg 86, 89
Damian Wayne 51, 73, 75
    see also Robin
Dark Knight 4–5, 18, 26, 28, 35, 41, 45, 47, 49, 53, 55, 56, 61, 63, 67, 68–69, 70, 77, 82, 84
    see also Batman
Darkseid 86
Dick Grayson 74, 80–81, 91
    see also Robin, Nightwing, Agent 37
Dr. Francine Langstrom 67
    see also Bat-Queen
Dr. Harleen Quinzel 42
    see also Harley Quinn
Dr. Kirk Langstrom 66–67
    see also Man-Bat
Edward Nygma 58 see also The Riddler
Fear Toxin 49, 56, 69
Firefly 21
Gotham City 4, 6–8, 10, 26, 28–29, 30–31, 33, 34–35, 36, 39, 40, 44–45, 46–47, 49, 52, 54, 56–57, 59, 62, 64, 68, 69, 73, 74, 76–77, 78–79, 83, 84–85
Gotham City Gazette 12–13
Gotham City Police Department 76–77
Green Lantern 86, 89
Hal Jordan 89 see also Green Lantern
Harley Quinn 37, 42–43, 91
Harper Row 85 see also Bluebird
Harvey Bullock 77
Harvey Dent 44–45 see also Two-Face
Hawkfire 85, 91
Jason Todd 74, 80
    see also Robin, Red Hood

Jeremiah Arkham 37
Jonathan Crane 56 *see also* Scarecrow
Justice League 86, 89, 91
Kal-El 88 *see also* Superman
Kate Kane 85 *see also* Batwoman
Killer Croc 38, 64–65
Krypton 88
Lazarus Pits 50
Lex Luthor 86
League of Assassins 50
Lucius Fox 85
Luke Fox 85
Mad Hatter 38
Man-Bat 66–67
Martha Wayne 7
Matches Malone 15
Maxie Zeus 38
Mr Freeze 21, 37, 39, 62–63
Nightwing 74, 80
Oswald Cobblepot 46
          see also The Penguin
Pamela Isley 48 *see also* Poison Ivy
Paradise Island 88
Poison Ivy 5, 37, 43, 48–49, 59, 85
Queen Hippolyta 88
Rā's al Ghūl 16, 50–51, 69, 75, 85
Red Hood 74
Red Hood Gang 10, 40, 58
Red Robin 75
Renee Montoya 77
Robin 5, 31, 73, 74–75
Selina Kyle 78 *see also* Catwoman

Sergei Alexandrov 9
Shihan Matsuda 9
Spyral 81
Superman 86, 88
Talia al Ghūl 51, 73, 75
Talons 54–55, 69
The Flash 86, 89
The Heretic 73
The Joker 5, 16, 23, 36, 37,
          38, 40–41, 42, 43, 53, 59,
          68, 82
The Penguin 5, 46–47
The Riddler 58–59, 85
The Scarecrow 36, 38, 49, 56–57
The Spectre 39
Themiscyra 88
Thomas Wayne 7
Tim Drake 74, 75, 80
          see also Robin, Red Robin
Two-Face 38, 44–45
Utility Belt 22, 23, 24
Venom 52, 68
Victor Fries 62 *see also* Mr. Freeze
Victor Stone 89 *see also* Cyborg
Victor Zsasz 39
Waylon Jones 64
          see also Killer Croc
Wayne Enterprises 6, 16, 32, 48,
          58, 62
Wayne Manor 32, 39, 70
Wonder Woman 86, 88
Zeus 88

Quiz answers
1. The murder of his parents.
2. Shihan Matsuda and Sergei Alexandrov 3. Matches Malone
4. The Joker 5. 1,000lb
6. Damian Wayne 7. Titanium and Kevlar 8. Tyrannosaurus Rex
9. £30million ($46million)
10. An oversized mallet
11. The Court of Owls
12. He lights up the Bat-Signal
13. Spyral 14. She is her cousin.
15. Darkseid

Have you read these other great books from DK?

Read all about the scariest monsters in the Star Wars galaxy.

Join the mighty Avengers as they battle the power-mad robot Ultron!

Find out all about the brave Jedi Knights and their epic adventures.

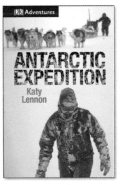

Discover how to survive in the most hostile place on Earth—Antarctica.

Enjoy the myths and legends from long ago and across the world.

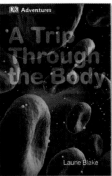

Explore the amazing systems at work inside the human body.